Summer Sips to "Chill" Dips

Yummy Tummy Recipes
SEASONS

by Marilyn LaPenta

Consultant:
Mandi Pek, MS, RD, CSP, CDN

BEARPORT PUBLISHING

NEW YORK, NEW YORK

Credits

All food illustrations by Kim Jones

Publisher: Kenn Goin
Editor: Joy Bean
Creative Director: Spencer Brinker
Design: Debrah Kaiser

Library of Congress Cataloging-in-Publication Data in process at time of publication (2013)
Library of Congress Control Number: 2012033939
ISBN-13: 978-1-61772-741-2 (library binding)

For more information, write to Bearport Publishing Company, Inc., 45 West 21st Street, Suite 3B, New York, New York, 10010. Printed in the United States of America.

10 9 8 7 6 5 4 3 2 1

Contents

Making Healthy Summer Treats

Get ready to make some super yummy summer treats! The refreshing creations in *Summer Sips to "Chill" Dips* use fresh food in really simple recipes.

In the summer, fresh fruits and vegetables are inexpensive and plentiful. The best of this **seasonal produce** is available at farmers' markets or small family farms. These places offer locally grown fruits and veggies that have just been picked. This kind of produce usually has more nutritional value than food that is chilled for weeks and shipped long distances.

The great thing about making your own summer drinks and dips is that you know exactly what goes into each recipe. Many **pre-made** foods contain **preservatives** that are not always good for your body. Use the ideas on page 22 for making the nutritious drinks and dips in this book even healthier.

Getting Started

Use these cooking tips and safety and tool guidelines to make the best drinks and dips you've ever tasted.

Tips

Here are a few tips to get your cooking off to a great start.

- Quickly check out the Prep Time, Tools, and Servings information at the top of each recipe. It will tell you how long the recipe takes to prepare, the tools you'll need, and the number of people the recipe serves.

- Once you pick a recipe, set out the tools and ingredients that you will need on your worktable.

- Before and after cooking, wash your hands well with warm soapy water to kill any germs.

- Wash all fruits and vegetables, as appropriate, to get rid of any dirt and chemicals.

- Put on an apron or smock to protect your clothes.

- Roll up long shirtsleeves to keep them clean.

- Tie back long hair or cover it to keep it out of the food.

- *Very Important:* Keep the adults happy by cleaning up the kitchen when you've finished cooking.

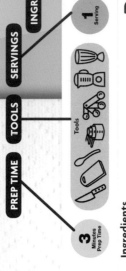

PREP TIME **TOOLS** **SERVINGS**

INGREDIENT

1 Serving

3 Minutes Prep Time

Tools

RECIPE

Ingredients

1 ripe avocado (soft to the touch)

1 cup **low-fat** or skim milk

1 cup ice

½ teaspoon vanilla extract

1 tablespoon honey or agave

Optional: mint

Steps

1. Ask an adult to cut the avocado in half with the knife on the cutting board. Remove the pit and throw it away. With the spoon, scrape out the green **flesh** of the fruit from the **rind** and put it into the blender.

2. Pour the rest of the ingredients into the blender.

3. **Blend** on high for 30 seconds or until smooth.

4. Pour the mixture into the glass.

5. Add a sprig of mint if desired for decoration.

Avocados are in the Guinness Book of World Records as the most nutritious fruit known to man.

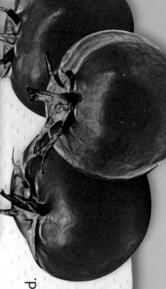

Be Safe

Cook safely by having an adult around to help with these activities:

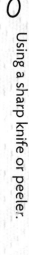

Using a sharp knife or peeler.

Using the stove, the blender, or other electrical appliances.

Removing hot pans from the oven. (Always use pot holders.)

Frying foods on top of the stove. (Keep the heat as low as possible to avoid burns from oil splatter.)

Tools You Need

Here's a guide to the tools you will need to make the various recipes in this book.

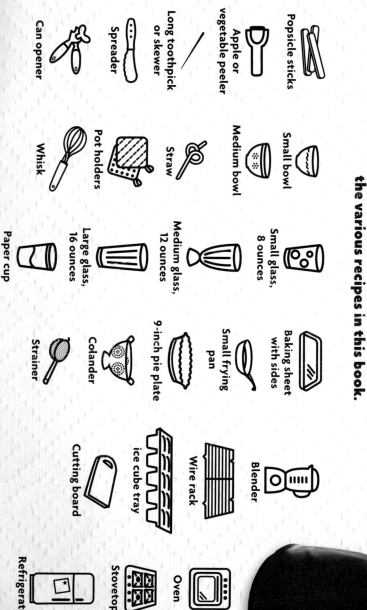

Mixing spoon

Spoon

Knife

Fork

Measuring spoons

Measuring cups

Popsicle sticks

Apple or vegetable peeler

Spreader

Long toothpick or skewer

Can opener

Small bowl

Medium bowl

Straw

Pot holders

Whisk

Small glass, 8 ounces

Medium glass, 12 ounces

Large glass, 16 ounces

Paper cup

Baking sheet with sides

Small frying pan

9-inch pie plate

Colander

Strainer

Blender

Wire rack

ice cube tray

Cutting board

Oven

Stovetop

Refrigerator

Peach Raspberry Shake

5 Minutes Prep Time

2 Servings

Ingredients

1 peach

6 ounces **low-fat** vanilla yogurt

½ cup raspberries

Tools

8 ice cubes

Optional: a few extra raspberries for decoration

Steps

1. Ask an adult to use the knife to cut the peach in half on the cutting board and **slice** its **flesh** off the pit. Throw out the pit.

2. Put the peach, yogurt, raspberries, and ice cubes into the blender. **Blend** on high for 30 seconds.

3. Pour the mixture into the glasses.

4. If desired, decorate with a few raspberries threaded onto a long toothpick.

Raspberries come in four colors: black, red, purple, and gold.

Health Tip

Raspberries are a very healthy snack. They contain large amounts of **fiber** and **vitamins**, such as C, E, and K.

Mango Berry Creamsicle

5 Minutes Prep Time

Tools

2 Servings

Ingredients

1 cup fresh pre-cut mango, cut into 1-inch cubes

1 cup fresh strawberries, cut in half

¾ cup mango **sorbet**

1 cup orange juice

Optional: 1 tablespoon shredded coconut

Steps

1. If you are not using a pre-cut mango, ask an adult to use the knife to **slice** the mango in half on the cutting board and remove the pit. Have him or her cut lines into each half of the fruit's flesh in a checkerboard pattern, without cutting through the skin. Gently push on the mango skin, and the cubes inside will pop up—ready to be sliced off.

2. Remove the stems and leaves from the strawberries. Then cut the berries in half.

3. Put the mango, strawberries, sorbet, and juice into the blender.

4. **Blend** on high for 45 seconds or until smooth.

5. Pour the mixture into the two glasses.

6. Sprinkle the shredded coconut on top if desired.

The mango is one of the most commonly eaten fruits in tropical countries around the world. In fact, more mangos are eaten every day than any other fruit in the world.

Cool Green Smoothie

3 Minutes Prep Time

1 Serving

Tools

Ingredients

1 ripe avocado (soft to the touch)

1 cup **low-fat** or skim milk

1 cup ice

½ teaspoon vanilla extract

1 tablespoon honey or agave

Optional: mint

Steps

1. Ask an adult to use the knife to cut the avocado in half on the cutting board. Remove the pit and throw it away. With the spoon, scrape out the green **flesh** of the fruit from the **rind** and put it into the blender.

2. Pour the rest of the ingredients into the blender.

3. **Blend** on high for 30 seconds or until smooth.

4. Pour the mixture into the glass.

5. Add a sprig of mint if desired for decoration.

Avocados are in the Guinness Book of World Records as the most nutritious fruit known to man.

Watermelon Lemonade

10 Minutes Prep Time

Tools

6 Servings

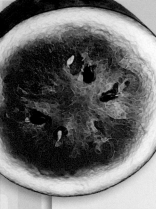

Ingredients

¼ cup water

¼ cup sugar

2 cups seedless watermelon

1½ cups cold water

¼ cup lemon juice (fresh or from concentrate)

3 cups ice

Steps

1. Pour the water and sugar into the frying pan and place the pan on the stovetop. With an adult's help, let the mixture **boil** over medium heat until the sugar dissolves, stirring frequently with the spoon (about 5 minutes).

2. With the pot holder, carefully remove the pan from the heat and let it cool.

3. Using the knife, cut the watermelon into 1-inch cubes on the cutting board.

4. Put the watermelon into the blender. **Blend** on high for 30 seconds or until smooth.

5. Put the cold water, lemon juice, and cooled mixture from the frying pan into the blender. Blend on high for another 10 seconds.

6. Put ½ cup of ice in each of the glasses. Pour the mixture over the ice.

Watermelon pickers know a watermelon is ripe when they can see a creamy yellow spot on the bottom of the fruit. The spot indicates where the watermelon sat on the ground.

Health Tip

Watermelon can boost your energy level because it has a high amount of vitamin B, which supplies our bodies with natural energy.

Strawberry Sensation

3 Minutes Prep Time

1 Serving

Tools

Ingredients

¼ cup **low-fat** milk

1 6-ounce cup blueberry yogurt

1 frozen banana, peeled

5 large strawberries with their stems removed

Optional: 1 whole strawberry for decoration

Steps

1. Put all the ingredients into the blender in the order listed above.

2. **Blend** for 45 seconds or until the banana is blended smoothly into the drink.

3. Pour the mixture into the tall glass.

4. Add a whole strawberry to the glass rim for decoration if desired.

The strawberry is not classified as a true berry like the blueberry or the cranberry because it does not have seeds on the inside. The seeds of the strawberry are on the outside.

Health Tip

Strawberries are very low in **calories**. One cup of unsweetened strawberries has only 55 calories.

Berry Melon Mint Pops

Tools

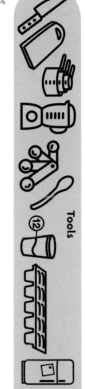

Ingredients

4 cups seedless watermelon, cut into 1-inch cubes

¼ cup mint leaves

¼ cup raspberries

2 tablespoons honey

2 teaspoons fresh lemon juice

½ cup blueberries

Steps

1. Have an adult use the knife to cut the watermelon into 1-inch cubes on the cutting board. Throw away the **rind**.

2. Ask an adult to help **chop** the mint into tiny pieces.

3. Put the watermelon and the raspberries into the blender. Add the honey and the lemon juice and **blend** on high for 30 seconds.

4. Shut off the blender and remove the pitcher from the base. With the spoon, gently stir in the mint.

5. Pour the mixture into the cups or an ice cube tray and put in the freezer.

6. After about 1½ hours, drop blueberries on top of the pops. Then insert Popsicle sticks or small plastic spoons into the middle of the mixture.

7. When the pops are fully frozen (about 4 hours), remove the tray or cups from the freezer. Run under warm water for 5 seconds, and gently slide out the Popsicles.

The first Popsicle was created by accident in 1905 by an eleven-year-old boy names Frank Epperson. He left a homemade soda mixture outside on a cold night and found a frozen treat the next morning.

Health Tip

Watermelon rinds are **edible** and loaded with **vitamins** and other nutrients that people need.

Rainbow Kebabs

15 Minutes Prep Time

6 Servings

Tools

Ingredients

A selection of fruits:

Red: 6 whole washed strawberries or 6 1-inch pieces of watermelon

Orange: mango or cantaloupe cut into 6 1-inch pieces

Yellow: pineapple cut into 6 1-inch pieces or 6 ½-inch slices of banana

Green: honeydew melon cut into 6 1-inch pieces or peeled kiwi sliced into 6 ½-inch pieces or 6 whole green seedless grapes

Blue: 6 whole blueberries

Purple: 6 whole purple seedless grapes

6 ounces vanilla **low-fat** yogurt

1 teaspoon honey

¼ teaspoon lemon juice

Steps

1. Ask an adult to use the knife to cut the fruit, except for the berries and grapes, into bite-size pieces on the cutting board. Put each color of fruit in its own small bowl.

2. Select a piece of fruit from each bowl. Poke the **skewer** through the fruit pieces, arranging the fruit on the skewer in the order of the colors of the rainbow: red, orange, yellow, green, blue, and purple.

3. Use the spoon to mix the yogurt, honey, and lemon juice together in a small bowl.

4. Dip the fruit into the mixture as you eat it.

Unlike some fruits, blueberries and grapes don't ripen after they are picked.

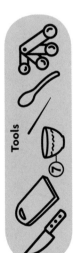

14

Fourth of July Red, White, and Blue Chips

15 Minutes Prep Time

10 Minutes Cooking Time

Tools

6 Servings

Ingredients

1 bag (about 6 ounces) blue corn tortilla chips

6 ounces Monterey jack cheese, shredded

6 ounces store-bought salsa (mild, medium, or hot according to your taste) or homemade salsa (page 18)

6 ounces **low-fat** sour cream

Steps

1. **Preheat** the oven to 350°F.

2. Cover the baking sheet with large blue corn tortilla chips.

3. Sprinkle the cheese over the chips.

4. Bake in the oven for 10 minutes.

5. Carefully remove the baking sheet from the oven with the pot holders.

6. Drop spoonfuls of salsa over the cheese-covered chips.

7. Top each spot of salsa with a ½ teaspoon of low-fat sour cream.

8. Eat immediately!

The blue color found in blue corn tortilla chips comes from anthocyanins, which are the same healthy compounds found in blue and purple foods such as blueberries and eggplants.

Health Tip

Blue corn tortilla chips have less **starch** and more **protein** than white corn tortilla chips.

Seven-Layer Dip

Health Tip

A serving of refried beans has about 13 grams of **protein**.

20 Minutes Prep Time

Tools

12 Servings

Ingredients

1 large tomato

½ cup sliced green onions

1 small can (about 2 ounces) sliced or chopped black olives

1 cup **low-fat** sour cream

1 package (about 1 ounce) of taco seasoning mix

3 ripe avocados (soft to the touch)

3 tablespoons lemon juice

1 16-ounce can refried beans

1 cup shredded cheddar cheese

Baked tortilla chips

Steps

1. Ask an adult to use the knife to **dice** the tomato and the green onions on the cutting board.

2. Open the can of olives. Use the strainer to drain off the liquid into the sink.

3. With the spoon, mix the sour cream and taco seasoning in a small bowl until well blended. Then clean the spoon.

4. Cut the avocados in half with the knife and remove the pits. With the spoon, scoop out the green **flesh** from the **rind** and put it in the other small bowl. Add the lemon juice. With the fork, mash the avocado and lemon juice together.

5. Open the can of refried beans. Spread the beans on the bottom of the pie plate with the spreader.

6. Clean the spreader. Then spread the sour cream mixture over the beans. Clean the spreader again, and then spread the avocado mixture on top of the sour cream mixture.

7. Sprinkle the tomatoes on next, then the onions, then the olives. Top with the shredded cheese.

8. Serve with baked tortilla chips.

The only difference between green olives and black olives is ripeness. Green olives are not ripe, and black olives are fully ripe.

Spinach Hummus Dip

Ingredients

½ cup fresh spinach, washed

15 ounces garbanzo beans (chickpeas), drained

2 tablespoons chopped garlic

2 tablespoons olive oil

3 tablespoons lemon juice

¼ cup water

¼ teaspoon salt

¼ cup **tahini** or peanut butter

For dipping: your favorite vegetables washed and cut into strips or bite-size pieces; or pita bread cut into small triangles

Steps

1. Rip the spinach leaves into small pieces.

2. Ask an adult to help you open the can of chickpeas. Use the strainer to drain off the liquid into the sink. Do not rinse the chickpeas.

3. Put the spinach, beans, garlic, olive oil, lemon juice, water, and salt into the blender. **Blend** on high for 1 minute or until smooth.

4. Add the tahini to the mixture in the blender. Blend for another minute or until creamy.

5. Serve with cut-up vegetables or pita bread.

Spinach is a strong crop and can grow in temperatures as low as 20 degrees Fahrenheit.

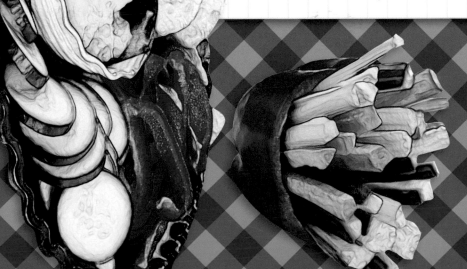

Health Tip

Instead of spinach, you may use any kind of green leafy vegetable in this recipe for a different flavor: broccoli rabe, kale, collard greens, etc.

Simple Salsa

Health Tip

If you use fresh garlic and fresh lime juice in your salsa, it will help to prevent the growth of bacteria.

15 Minutes Prep Time*

* Plus 1 Hour to Chill

6 Servings

Tools

Ingredients

⅓ cup cucumber

2 cups tomatoes

½ cup red onion

½ cup fresh basil

1 hot red pepper with seeds removed

¼ teaspoon salt

2 tablespoons lime juice

Baked tortilla chips

Steps

1. Ask an adult for help with peeling and cutting. Then use the peeler to peel the cucumber.

2. Use the knife to cut the tomatoes, cucumber, and red onion into ¼-inch pieces on the cutting board.

3. **Chop** the basil and the hot red pepper.

4. In the bowl, combine the cucumber, onion, tomatoes, basil, hot pepper, salt, and lime juice. Stir with the spoon.

5. Chill for 1 hour in the refrigerator.

6. Serve with baked tortilla chips.

Tomatoes and jalapeño peppers are actually fruits, not vegetables. Salsa is the Spanish word for sauce.

18

Light Cucumber Dip

5
Minutes
Prep Time*

*Plus 2 Hours to Chill

Tools

6
Servings

Ingredients

1 cup Greek yogurt

½ cup chopped cucumber

½ cup chopped red onion

2 tablespoons chopped fresh chives

1 tablespoon chopped fresh parsley

1 tablespoon fresh dill weed

Cherry tomatoes or a variety of your favorite vegetables cut into strips or pieces for dipping

Steps

1. In a small bowl combine the yogurt, cucumber, onion, chives, parsley, and dill.

2. Mix all the ingredients with a spoon until blended.

3. Chill the mixture for 2 hours in the refrigerator.

4. Serve with cherry tcmatoes or your favorite vegetables cut into bite-size pieces for dipping.

For any recipe, you may use fresh or dried herbs. If you use dried herbs, reduce the amount by at least half.

Health Tip

Cucumber is very popular in facial treatments because, when it is applied to the skin, it cools the blood and eases facial swelling.

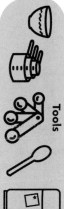

Zucchini Chips

 15 Minutes Prep Time

 **30** Minutes Cooking Time

 **6** Servings

Tools

Ingredients

¼ cup plain bread crumbs

½ cup Parmesan cheese (fresh or packaged)

¼ teaspoon salt

⅛ teaspoon pepper

¼ teaspoon paprika

3 tablespoons **low-fat** milk

Cooking spray

2 ½ cups zucchini cut into ¼-inch rounds (about 2 medium zucchini)

Steps

1 **Preheat** the oven to 425°F.

2 With the whisk, mix the bread crumbs, cheese, salt, pepper, and paprika in a small bowl.

3 Pour the milk into another small bowl.

4 Place the wire rack on a baking sheet and lightly coat it with the cooking spray.

5 Dip each slice of zucchini in the milk and then in the bread crumbs mixture, covering both sides, and place on the wire rack.

6 Cook for 30 minutes or until brown and crisp. Carefully remove the tray from the oven with a pot holder. Eat while warm.

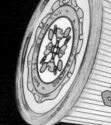

Health Tip

One cup of zucchini has only 20 **calories** and 5 percent of our daily **fiber** needs.

The flower of the zucchini plant is also edible.

Black Bean and Corn Dip

15 Minutes Prep Time

Tools

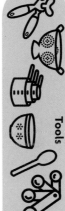

10 Servings

Ingredients

1 15-ounce can black beans

1 15-ounce can white kernel corn (or 2 cups frozen corn)

1 large tomato, cut into ¼-inch pieces

1 purple onion, chopped

1 tablespoon cumin powder

1 tablespoon cilantro or parsley

1 teaspoon garlic, peeled and chopped

2 tablespoons fresh lime juice

Baked tortilla chips

Steps

1. Ask an adult to use the can opener to open the cans of black beans and corn.

2. Place the colander in the sink. Pour in the contents of the cans to drain the liquid.

3. Put the beans and corn in the medium mixing bowl and stir together with the mixing spoon.

4. Add the tomato, onion, cumin, cilantro, and garlic.

5. Add the lime juice and stir all the ingredients together with the mixing spoon until the mixture is well blended.

6. Serve the dip immediately or chill it in the refrigerator for up to a day.

7. Serve with baked tortilla chips.

A serving of black beans has about ten times more antioxidants than a serving of oranges.

Health Tip

Black beans are very high in **fiber, protein,** and **antioxidants,** along with other **vitamins** and **minerals.**

Nutrition Facts

Serving Size 5 oz. (144g)
Servings Per Container 4

Amount Per Serving		
Calories 310	Calories from Fat 100	
		% Daily Value*
Total Fat 15g		21%
Saturated Fat 2.6g		17%
Trans Fat 1g		
Cholesterol 118mg		39%
Sodium 560mg		28%
Total Carbohydrate 12g		4%
Dietary Fiber 1g		4%
Sugars 1g		
Protein 24g		

Vitamin A 1%	•	**Vitamin C** 2%
Calcium 2%	•	**Iron** 5%

*Percent Daily Values are based on a 2,000 calorie diet. Your daily values may be higher or lower depending on your calorie needs:

	Calories	2,000	2,500
Total Fat	Less Than	65g	80g
Saturated Fat	Less Than	20g	25g
Cholesterol	Less Than	300mg	300mg
Sodium	Less Than	2,400mg	2,400mg
Total Carbohydrate		300g	375g
Dietary Fiber		25g	30g

Calories 4 • Protein 4

Healthy Tips

Always Read Labels

Labels tell how much fat, sugar, **vitamins**, and other nutrients are in food. If you compare one bottle of juice with another, for example, you can determine which one has fewer **calories**, less sugar, and so on. Don't forget to look at the serving size when comparing foods.

Make Recipe Substitutions

While all the recipes in this book call for wholesome ingredients, you can make even healthier snacks by substituting some ingredients for others. For example:

🥄 Dairy: use nonfat or **low-fat** instead of full fat when it comes to dairy products such as yogurt, cheese, sour cream, and milk.

🥄 Chips: choose chips that are baked.

🥄 Salt: choose "lightly salted" or "no salt added" chips to reduce **sodium** content.

🥄 Juice: choose 100 percent fruit juice, or juice with no added sugar.

🥄 Sugar: use honey or agave instead of sugar.

🥄 Herbs: use fresh herbs for better taste and nutrition. If using dry herbs, reduce the amount called for in the recipe by at least a half.

Glossary

antioxidants (an-tee-OK-suh-duhnts) substances in certain foods that may prevent cell damage, which can cause disease

blend (BLEND) to mix two or more ingredients together

boil (BOIL) to heat a liquid until it starts to bubble

calories (KAL-uh-reez) measurements of the amount of energy that food provides

chop (CHOP) to cut something into small pieces

dice (DICE) to cut something into small cubes

edible (ED-uh-buhl) able to be eaten

fiber (FYE-bur) a substance found in parts of plants that when eaten passes through the body but is not completely digested; it helps food move through one's intestines and is important for good health

flesh (FLESH) the part of a fruit or vegetable that is eaten

low-fat (loh-FAT) food that has three or fewer grams of fat per serving

minerals (MIN-ur-uhlz) chemical substances, such as iron and zinc, that occur naturally in certain foods and are important for good health

preheat (PREE-heet) to turn on an oven and allow it to heat up to a specific temperature before using

pre-made (PREE-mayd) already prepared

preservatives (pri-ZUR-vuh-tivz) chemicals put into foods to keep them from spoiling

produce (pruh-DOOSS) fruits and vegetables

protein (PROH-teen) a substance found in plants and animals that the human body needs in order to build and repair muscle, skin, nails, and hair. It can be found in cheese, yogurt, eggs, fish, meat, beans, and other foods

rind (RIND) the tough outer skin of certain fruits

seasonal (SEE-sun-al) relating to a particular season of the year

skewer (SKYOO-ur) a long, thin piece of metal or wood used to hold meat and vegetables while they are being cooked

slice (SLYES) to cut into thin, flat pieces

sodium (SOH-dee-uhm) a chemical found in salt that the body needs in small amounts; too much salt in one's diet can cause health problems

sorbet (sor-BAY) a frozen dessert made with fruit juice

starch (STARCH) a white substance found in foods such as potatoes and bananas

tahini (tuh-HEE-nee) a sesame seed paste

vitamins (VYE-tuh-minz) substances in food that are necessary for good health

23

Index

Bibliography

Karmel, Annabel. *Mom and Me Cookbook: Have Fun in the Kitchen.* New York: DK (2009).

Wilenski, Amy. *Healthy Snacks for Kids: Recipes for Nutritious Bites at Home or on the Go.* Guilford, CT: Knack (2010).

Read More

Graimes, Nicola. *Kids' Fun and Healthy Cookbook.* New York: Dorling Kindersley (2007).

Low, Jennifer. *Kitchen for Kids: 100 Amazing Recipes Your Children Can Really Make.* Canada: Whitecap Books (2010).

Learn More Online

To learn more about making summer sips and 'chill' dips, visit **www.bearportpublishing.com/YummyYummyRecipes-Seasons**

About the Author

Marilyn LaPenta has been a teacher for more than 25 years and has published numerous works for teachers and students. She has always enjoyed cooking with her students and her three children, and looks forward to cooking with her three grandchildren. Marilyn lives in Brightwaters, New York.